on the train

Carron Brown

Illustrated by Bee Johnson

A DIVISION OF EDC PUBLISHING

A railroad station is bustling with activity.

If you peer between the engines in the sheds, through the cars and down the platforms, you can see different kinds of trains.

Shine a flashlight behind the page, or hold it up to the light to find engineers, maintenance workers, passengers, and freight. Discover a world of great surprises.

Before they travel, the trains are checked
and tested by maintenance workers.

Can you see what happens
in the blue shed?

This engine is moving through a train wash.

Spinning rollers cover it with soap
and water to make it sparkle.

Swish!

Swish!

Splish!

This train's windows are cleaned before its next trip.

Can you see another busy maintenance worker?

Glug! Glug!

This train runs on fuel called diesel.

The maintenance worker connects the fuel pump to
the train and fills the tank with diesel.

All aboard!

The conductor on the platform is blowing his whistle to let the engineer know it's safe to go.

Who is checking the tickets?

Click! Clack!

This conductor checks each ticket and
then punches a hole in it.

Passengers can also ask the conductor
questions about the trip.

The doors close and our train moves out of the station.

Take a peek inside the engineer's cab.

Whoosh!

The engineer pushes the
speed control.

This makes the train
travel faster—around
100 miles per hour.

Rumble!
Rumble!

Our train stops
at a red signal.

A freight train rolls by.
Can you see what's
inside the freight cars?

Brrrr!

These containers are cold to keep
food fresh. There are onions from
a farm and fish from the sea.

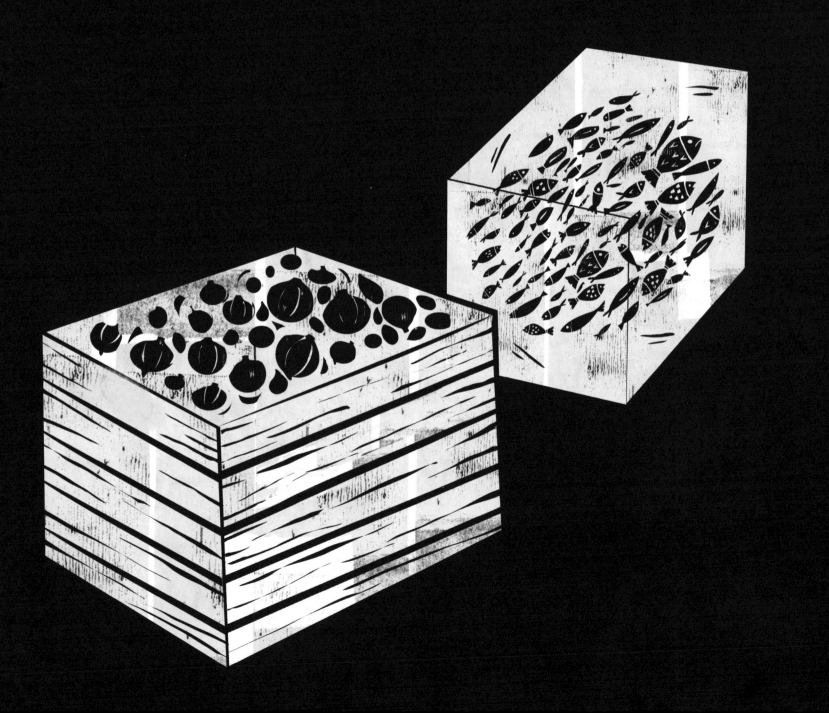

Look out the window. Behind the hill
smoke billows from a faraway train.

What kind
of train
makes smoke?

A steam engine high up on a viaduct.

Pufff!

Pufff!

A viaduct is a long, high bridge
that crosses over a valley or a river.

The engine burns coal to make
steam. Let's peek inside...

Whooosh!

The steam rushes out of the boiler
and pushes the pistons that turn
the engine's wheels.

This is an electric train
coming out of a tunnel.

Where does the electricity
come from?

Zzzzip!

Crackle!

A metal rod, called a pantograph, reaches
up and slides along overhead wires.

Electricity runs down the
pantograph to power the train.

Our train is changing direction.

Can you see why?

Maintenance workers wearing hard hats are fixing the rails.

A machine helps them lay new tracks in the right place.

Clank!

Clank!

Our train stops at a station. A porter rolls a food cart onto the train.

What are people doing in this car?

Eating!

This is the dining car. Here passengers
sit down for a meal or a drink.

The green train has stopped to let the passenger train pass by.

What are people doing in the white train?

Sleeping...

Ssshhh!

Passengers sleep in compartments with
beds. The train travels through the night.

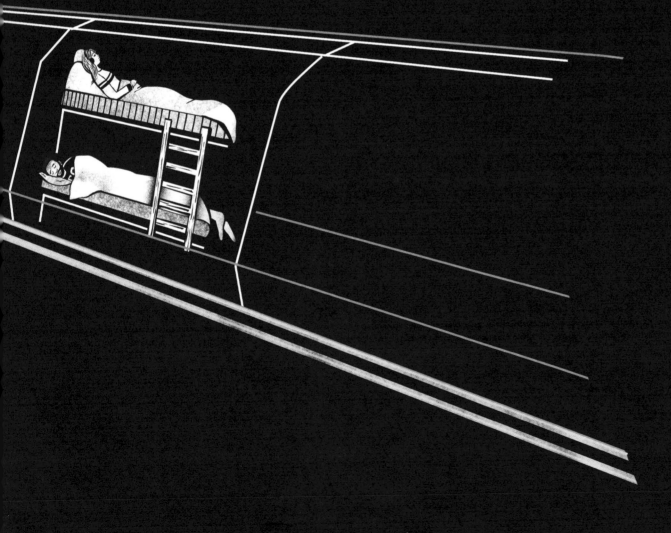

Honk! Honk!

A train sounds its horn as it travels through a town.

What's on the other side of the track?

Cars and people wait by a railroad crossing.

Vroom!
Vroom!

The gate will rise
when it is safe to cross.

The conductor on our train announces the
last stop. People stand up and get ready to leave.

What's inside their luggage?

Meow!

Some pets can travel on trains, too.
Cats go in special carriers.

Our train arrives in the city. We will get off this train and travel on an underground train, instead...

Clickety-clack!

Underground trains run under
the city through long tunnels.

It's a fast way to travel from
one part of town to another.

Our train uses its brakes to stop in the station.

What else can stop the train?

Buffers help stop the train.
They show the end of the line.

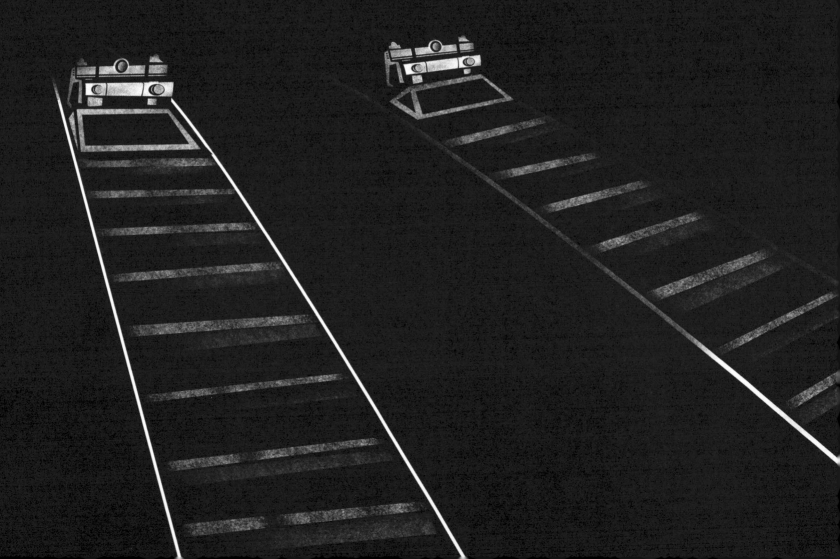

Our trip is over.
We have to leave our train.

Soon it will be time to
travel again. All aboard!

There's more...

When you are at a station or inside a car near a window, see how many types of trains you can find.

Passenger trains Fast trains carry people from one place to another. A conductor checks tickets and looks after passengers on board. In some countries, there are double-decker cars, with seats on two levels.

Freight trains have containers full of freight. Look out for different containers, such as an open-top car for coal, a tanker for gas, and a flat car for logs. Some freight trains can be several miles long.

Underground trains Some cities have an underground railroad or subway that takes people from one place in the city to another through tunnels. Each city has a special railway map with all the stations marked.

Maglevs Magnetic levitation (maglev) trains hover and glide above a track. They are held in place by strong magnets. The maglev trains in Shanghai, China, are the fastest in the world. They can reach 310 miles per hour (500 kilometers per hour).

Monorail trains run along one rail. Monorail trains are found in cities, especially in airports, and take people on short trips. Some monorail trains hang down from a rail, with their wheels on the roof.

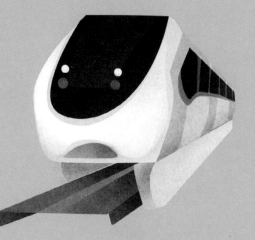

Overnight trains People travel through the night on trains that have cars with compartments with beds to sleep in. Passengers can eat meals in a dining car. Some overnight trains travel between cities in one country and others travel from one country to another.

Steam trains The first trains were powered by steam made from burning coal in an engine. Steam trains still run today, but most travel for short distances and are used by tourists. They are slower than modern trains.

Trams Trains that run on rails along city streets are called trams. They sometimes share the road with other vehicles. The rails are often sunk into the street so that people do not trip over them when crossing the road.

First American Edition 2015
Kane Miller, A Division of EDC Publishing

Copyright © 2015 The Ivy Press Limited

Published by arrangement with Ivy Press Limited, United Kingdom.

For information contact:
Kane Miller, A Division of EDC Publishing
PO Box 470663
Tulsa, OK 74147-0663
www.kanemiller.com
www.edcpub.com
www.usbornebooksandmore.com

Library of Congress Control Number: 2014947161

Printed in China

ISBN: 978-1-61067-365-5